The Truth About
Acting

How Acting and Spirituality
fuse to propel you

Tula Tzoras

BALBOA.
PRESS

A DIVISION OF HAY HOUSE

Balboa Press books may be ordered through booksellers or by contacting:

Balboa Press
A Division of Hay House
1663 Liberty Drive
Bloomington, IN 47403
www.balboapress.com.au
1-(877) 407-4847

ISBN: 978-1-4525-1055-2 (sc)
ISBN: 978-1-4525-1054-5 (e)

Balboa Press rev. date: 07/12/2013

Contents

Introduction

Life is not a rehearsal; we only have one chance at it. My name is Tula Tzoras and I am a working Actor, TV Presenter, Director and Producer. I have spent my adult life in the Entertainment Industry and if I was given a choice right now, I wouldn't change a thing.

My journey as an Actor has been one of elation and despair. I have had adventures, worked with incredible people, travelled to far cities and toured to small towns. I have studied human nature and in turn my own nature. To do that I have gone on a personal growth journey to overcome my past limitations. This path has included becoming a Reiki Master, experimenting with other healing modalities like Chinese medicine, re-birthing, energetic healing and taking part in inner child workshops. I took courses in emotional intelligence and conflict resolution. I also studied Buddhist meditation and completed a program on relationships. I have attended many Inspirational Seminars and helped others however I could. I have read many books and practice meditation daily. My path as an Actor has been deeply spiritual.

The benefit of having such a varied personal education has been that I have been able to take something from all these disciplines and develop my own philosophy. The most amazing gift however, has been learning who I am, becoming authentic and learning how to love myself, something all Artists need to do, because as Artists we live in uncertainty. I have learnt to practice self-referral, which in my opinion is the difference between heaven and hell and heaven and hell are right here in our very own brains.

My decision to write this book was based on my motivation to share my experience and knowledge, so that you too may move from doubt to certainty, skip the trial and error I experienced and experience the success you deserve even sooner.

Lets start right now: Take deep, slow breaths . . .

This book is written for the Artist in You.

The Aim of this book is to sky rocket your success as an Actor. By giving you a holistic, powerful perspective towards acting. This book will empower you with your very own secret weapon. You will learn how to create the ideal formula for success. You will become a deliberate creator of your dreams and find out how The Laws of Success can transcend your experience as an Actor and put you in a state of creative inspiration.

So Breathe . . .

"The Truth About Acting" is a career biography for professional and personal development, because I believe your craft and your creative self go hand in hand. Using examples from the various challenges that I have faced and overcome in my own career, I will provide advice about the best response to those challenges. I will also canvas alternative options in order to help you make the best choice for your career—and your life, living in Certainty as a Creative Soul.

Firstly, I will share specific examples from the Industry, in the hope that my experience will give you the insight to make good choices. Whilst my journey was one of trial and error and personal growth spanning over a lifetime, you will have the opportunity to use the tools I provide for you straight away. Then you will be given your own secret weapon and the way to love auditions, rather than dread them! "The Truth About Acting" will prepare you in ways traditional training and literature does not. It will provide you with a healthy blueprint for your life as a whole, as you enjoy your creative expression.

Millions of people want to be rich and famous—or at the very least in some way glamorous. Fame is an attractive, addictive, albeit fickle pursuit for many people. Let me stress the word Fickle! How many stars have found peril paired with their loss of fame?

If you choose to be an Actor or an Artist, do it because you love the work. Anything you do from the space of Love will always feed your soul and line your pockets.

I hope that all the thousands of young actors entering the market every year can benefit from this realistic, yet supportive perspective on what it truly means to be an actor, a creative artist.

Acting is a Life Choice. You may have heard the expression "Character Building" and it is. Acting is food for the soul, a journey into the heart of humanity and imagination. A career in Acting is a true adventure, taking one out of the mediocre in to an extraordinary way of being. It is living in the magical world of possibility.

Acting demands persistence, however. It requires attention to detail, skill, imagination, vulnerability and hardness. The pursuit of truth in acting is a lifelong endeavour and there is nothing more rewarding than 'nailing' a character or a scene. To be an actor is to be rich and poor, rejected and accepted, applauded and slammed by reviews. As an Actor we are the product we are selling, the brand. We must ask ourselves, would we buy us?

Whilst most people will change careers or jobs a handful of times in their life span, actors go through auditions and contracts constantly by the thousands. Competition in this industry is fierce and requires one to be at the top of their game in every aspect of their being, whether it be our craft, physicality, energy, health, or life in general. We are a Brand!

In a lot of ways we are asked to be super human.

Having said that, it is obvious that a sound education at an accredited drama school is important. Support, both financial and emotional, is crucial. Proper training and solid support structures pave the path to a much easier passage into a career in acting. However, for many people, those aspects are not always within reach. That is where I come in!

Someone who has always been driven by blind ambition and determination wrote "The Truth About Acting". When I began my journey towards my dream, I didn't have the information I needed to enter into the industry. It was the 80s! I'd enjoyed ballet and piano lessons as a child and although I always knew I wanted to perform, I didn't have the tools to know how to go about it. I already knew I was a chameleon having attended approximately ten schools and having had to fit in as an outsider every time. All I knew was "Persistence Beats Resistance". That is how I began my career as an actor.

I hope "The Truth About Acting" gives you an insight into the world of acting and the potential impact it may have on your life. If my experiences can assist you in avoiding pitfalls like overdoing things and collapsing from Chronic Fatigue Syndrome, for instance, I will have reached my goal. If you practice your Secret Weapon and become Deliberate Creators of your Dreams, I will be over the moon for you! Most importantly when you practice Self Referral and move from Uncertainty into Certainty, you will experience Heaven on Earth. Nothing would make me happier!

I do hope you enjoy ". The Truth About Acting"

Chapter 1

The Early Years

Relevant snippets!

When my mum took me to school for the first time in Melbourne, all the kids were crying and holding on to their mothers in panic. I cheerfully waved goodbye to mum and off I went to class. She was shocked. That preceded a tendency to be fascinated by new and different things, sometimes forgetting the bell would ring, or forgetting the time on my way home and sending my mum crazy with worry. I somehow always managed to stand out in situations, although I was never aware of that. I lived in my imagination. I could see the magic in everything.

I remember my aunt Soula in Athens doing a card reading for me when I was a kid. She said I would walk through huge doors in my life, meaning I would be famous and powerful. That stayed with me. Who knows what future lay before me, but her thoughts inspired me.

My parents moved around a lot when I was young, so in my life I have attended around ten schools between two countries. I was forever the new kid on the block, trying to fit in and make friends. I took piano lessons and ballet. I loved dressing up. I used to spend hours in front of the mirrors in my mother's hairdressing salon making funny faces, until she had to remove the large one from the lunchroom. I became a chameleon.

Finally I went to University to study Arts and Drama, thanks to my conditioning. There was never anything I wanted to do more than perform. It was at University the fun really began.

Chapter 2

My First Taste

I always knew I wanted to perform. I knew I wanted to be an actor, a dancer. I wanted to go to drama school. When I was a child, Young Talent Time was a hit TV Show and I wanted to be on it! I nagged and nagged my parents. The only drama school I knew at the time was Rusden, which was a teacher's training college. I remember auditioning for them and doing some improvisations. Even though I had never done anything like that before, it was so exciting. We enacted a scene behind bars in a prison! I remember being elated that whole day.

My conservative background led me to Monash University to study Arts. My first choice was to enrol in English Literature and Drama. I was so lonely without my friends, but before I knew it I had joined several clubs and met lots of people. Being an A type personality I also took on a relationship and three other jobs.

At University I studied drama, relished in English Literature, modelled in fashion parades, played pool in the cafeteria, managed to be politically incorrect, take part in a demonstration and in the midst of it all seemed to forever need extensions on my assignments. In third year I needed to complete an entire year's work in a month in third term and managed to pass. This after a break up with my fiancé and a breakdown! A friend used to say if I ever got a degree it would be on how to beat the system. Of course doing so much had its impact and I was ill quite often.

I soon realised I suffered from anxiety and that was what drove me so much. I occasionally suffered panic attacks. They were so frightening I had no idea how to deal with them or the awareness to know what brought them on. The anxiety would give me great energy, even though it was uncomfortable. I looked into spiritual healing and started having Reiki sessions. Then I discovered Louise Hay's "You can heal your Life" and I dove straight into that. I found the affirmations so comforting. The explanations for different ailments came as a complete surprise to me. That was my first introduction to the mind/body relationship and metaphysics.

When I was studying, I also tutored, worked in a fashion boutique and did promotional work. A fellow student I met through the world of promotions, escorted me to a party one evening and introduced me to his agent. That night I felt his agent watch me, but I didn't' think twice about it. I had a great time meeting different people. I remember going to a lot of effort to look my best that evening. I felt good. That night I was the life of the party.

I was in the library trying to study when my friend came rushing in to see me. His agent wanted to meet me. I was thrilled. Finally, I thought to myself, my prayers had been answered and I would realise my dream of being an Actor.

I couldn't wait to meet this agent. I made an appointment straight away and saw him. He represented extras, but at that time I wasn't aware of the difference between being an extra and being an actor. He offered me representation and I jumped at it. He was the only person I had met in the industry. My first job happened quickly. I did an extras job to gain entry into the Actor's Union, Actor's Equity now the MEAA in Australia.

If you wanted to work in the industry, you had to be a member. That was a priority for me.

Then I waited. I waited and waited and waited. So much kept happening in my private life, my studies, my work, I could hardly keep up. The only area that stood still was the most important area of my life. My agent wasn't calling me with castings or work.

I didn't know how things worked then and I didn't know who to ask for help. Whenever I spoke with my agent he stalled.

Somehow he would put my mind at ease and this continued for some time. Finally I cornered him and all he said was "Persistence Beats Resistance".

Persistence beats Resistance. Persistence Beats Resistance.
Ok!

Suggested Choices

➢ Be very clear and focussed on your dream to become an Actor and ensure you receive the best education possible. Find out which courses are recognised and respected by the industry. This will make your journey easier, whilst your clarity and focus will make a clear statement to the Universe, about your intention.

➢ Research agencies before you join. Ensure the agency you join serves your career. You are the client. You can work with your agent to make strategic career choices. In theory your agent works for you, ideally however you will gain much more if you work as a team. Different agencies specialise in different areas, hence researching them will help you choose an agency that caters to your unique talent.

➢ If you wish to be considered as a serious actor, do not join an extras agency. Of course, extra work is a noble profession. If you do, however wish to be an actor, joining an extras agency will not serve your career because you will not be submitted for acting work.

➢ Keep up the work on your craft. Acting requires skill and technique and constant practice. Think of it as training to be an athlete. It is wise to receive the education and training you need.

➢ If you were the product you are selling, would you buy you? As Actors we are vessels for characters we play, therefore we are the product. Think of yourself as a brand, discover your unique talent, as we all have one and begin to work on reflecting that as a brand.

➢ It pays to do your homework. Research and learn the history of our craft. Know the great actors and their work. Know the great directors /producers and what they have done. Ensure you also know all the current players active in the industry and what they are doing at the moment, including actors, directors, and producers, casting agents.

➢ Attend all the networking events you can and mix with people in your industry. People always prefer working with people they like and whose work they are familiar with.

Networking is not a dirty word. Mixing with people of similar interests is a natural way to make friends!

➢ Market yourself. You are your own brand. Use the Internet, there are so many sites set up for Actors! Stay active and get the word out about what you are doing. Keep in touch.

➢ Always look your best and keep your skills honed. All these pieces combine to create your Brand.

➢ If you suffer from anxiety or any other physical or emotional illness, please ensure you are treated as soon as possible. Needless to say, alcohol, gambling, overeating or drugs are destructive. Quite often health issues can lead to addictive behaviours to cover feelings of suffering. Believe it or not, that can have a huge negative impact on your career, not to mention your life. How can you perform well if you are not well? Taking care of our selves is a gesture of love toward the self. That is a concept that is quite often foreign in our conditioning. Luckily, practice makes perfect.

➢ I suggest you start with a holistic approach to life if you wish to pursue acting or any creative path for that matter, because the choice you make when you pursue your creative dream, is to go into uncertainty, which is a perfect place to be, best served with good health, among other elements.

➢ Take up yoga and meditation and eat well. Work with inspirational and motivational material. You can make the choice to grow, get to know yourself and become your own best friend. One way of getting to know your self is to sit in silence, at least half an hour per day. "What does this have to do with acting", you may ask! If you were selling a product, wouldn't you wish to present it in a way that will sell? If you are in a supermarket, it may be the difference between organic produce and chemically treated produce, or free range eggs and cage eggs for example.

➢ Being authentic will be a huge asset to you. People immediately pick up on someone who is not being him or she. How does one become authentic, you may ask! The more you know and accept yourself, the more authentic you become and people will connect with you. Authenticity also follows acceptance for the self. The more we begin to accept our selves, the more comfortable we become in expressing who we are. How others perceive us then becomes less relevant. I invite you to take an inner journey to learn who you are.

➢ Performing, as a blank canvas will place you in the present, able to give the character you are playing freedom to make the best choices for the scene. When you are present you are also able to respond to direction. You are better able to listen. Think of yourself as a creative vessel. Shirley Maclaine is known for channelling her characters!

➢ We all have our own stories and crosses to bear. I will help you view those experiences as a positive and use them in your craft. This requires personal growth and development. That is why being in a Creative field is such a gift: it really is character building. We know life is full of opposite values: good and bad, cold and hot, joy and sorrow, pleasure and pain. If we treat each unwanted experience as a lesson, we see the gift in everything and the harmony of all that is. As you go through this book all the pieces will come together and make sense to you.

➢ Keep drama for the stage. If you keep your own stress to a minimum, you will enjoy life and your career immensely. So many people are addicted to drama. We have a choice to engage in it or not to engage in it. Dr Deepak Chopra says something like life is filled with a myriad of choices. Sometimes we do things so automatically we don't realise we are making a choice, but we are. If you begin to shift your focus to what you love and what makes you happy, you will find drama will be easy to turn away from.

➢ I recommend learning to love your self! "I am not selfish!" you may say indignantly. Loving yourself means thinking and doing nice things for and about your self. It means respect, non-judgement, forgiveness and all the nice things we often don't think we deserve. You can start with little things. If you begin to ask, "is this good for me?" when you make choices, you can trust that the feeling your body gives you when you ask will be right. Our bodies are amazing!

➤ A must: The Toltec Path to Freedom and The Four Agreements by Don Miguel Ruiz. The sooner you do this the better. The reason I recommend it for you is that it will help you in your practice of Self Referral! When you are an Artist, being subject to criticism, competition and judgement, Self Referral will do wonders for you. Self-Referral places you in your personal power. Allow me to explain: We each have our own spirit, soul and energetic field. It belongs to us. When we become aware of our personal feelings, what belongs to us and in turn what belongs to others, we are better able to separate the two. One of the benefits is we stop taking things personally. Can you see how that may benefit you as an Actor and Artist? And that is only one benefit of practising self-referral. It is the difference between heaven and hell in my humble opinion. The 7 Spiritual Laws of Success (Dr Deepak Chopra) are also a set of values to listen to daily and absorb organically. You can listen to the audio with your headphones as you travel! If you practise both, you will notice your career and life becoming lighter and easier and magic will begin to appear more and more often. You will find true freedom and I wish that for you.

➤ I suggest you learn to breathe deeply and slowly all the Time. Breathing deeply and slowly immediately stops you thinking! There are so many benefits of breathing deeply and slowly: it eliminates stress, connects you with the rhythm of the Universe, connects you with your source, infuses your cellular body with health giving oxygen, which in turn heals the body and last but not least, your creativity will flourish to your true potential! Esther and Jerry Hicks do some great 15 minute guided meditations to release resistance, i.e. getting out of your own way! Sounds good doesn't it? I can also recommend Kelly Howell's meditations. They work on the left and right brain and after 30 minutes of circular, divine, breathing, you will be buzzing from head to toe!

On location for "Party Poop" my second short film

Chapter 3

Persistence Beats Resistance

I was still working very hard and thinking Persistence Beats Resistance. I enrolled into an Actor's Workshop with a production company. We worked together for some time and then, before I knew it, I was asked to perform in a pilot they were shooting for a new series. I was over the moon. Paradoxically, as I was graduating from University, my entire life was falling apart. My fiancé gave me an ultimatum because there was a kissing scene in the pilot and I turned what I thought was the opportunity of a lifetime down.

It destroyed me emotionally but I thought I was choosing the man I loved. I was absolutely devastated for some time following that decision. At that time I learnt a very valuable lesson. Never again would I deny my own truth and my own work. I had to be accepted for who I was.

My first engagement ended in heartbreak and I was into my second engagement on the rebound, unbeknownst to me at the time. My second engagement ended. Meanwhile my second fiancé, in his real estate career, had ensured I became accustomed to a five star lifestyle, which only led me to delusions of grandeur and subsequent debt. In fact I was not only dealing with two failed engagements and bewildered parents, but also escalating debt, which kept me up at night. I was painfully thin.

Persistence Beats Resistance just stayed with me. I kept hearing it over and over in my head like a mantra. One day I simply decided to take matters into my own hands. In my limited knowledge of the industry, I only knew two Television production companies. In blind faith I would succeed, I called both companies to make appointments with their respective casting directors.

Whilst one company quickly obliged by offering me a general audition, the other casting director was too busy to contact. One day I heard the receptionist slip and divulge that casting director's whereabouts and an idea dawned on me like pure inspiration. I would dress up like a courier and personally deliver a small package with all my details to her at Channel Ten. In an absolute frenzy I got the package together and off I drove in my car.

I was very happy with myself until I reached the security gate. You are an actor I kept telling myself, you are playing the role of a courier. I told the security guard I had a package to deliver to the casting director. Then my stomach must have done a thousand summersaults when the guard announced she was on her way. SHE WAS ON HER WAY!

The Fear!

What would happen when she actually arrived? What would I have to say for myself? Luckily she was detained and I did manage to win a meeting with her. Mission Accomplished! I patted myself on the back. As I waited for my meeting with one Production Company and my audition with another, nothing else mattered.

*The Moomba Parade in Melbourne, Press Conference with Con
the Fruiterer as his daughter Toula*

Suggested Choices

➢ When you choose to be an actor, that is your job. As an actor you will be required to play many characters.

➢ As jobs are not usually an issue in relationships, I would advise you to choose a relationship with a person that understands what you do and supports your creativity as an artist. Love is about acceptance, the greatest gift of all.

➢ Arrange meetings or castings through your agent. If you don't have one, it is wise to arrange meetings in a preferred and professional manner.

➢ In my case, had I not taken matters into my own hands, my career would not have begun. It pays to be proactive in a constructive way. There is a fine line between being proactive and being inappropriate however.

➢ If you annoy casting people they will not wish to see you. If you waste their time they will simply not call you in for other roles.

➢ Once again, as much as possible, eliminate drama from your life, so that you have a clear platform to perform and not compounded stress to deal with.

➢ I recommend you listen to Dr Deepak Chopra's 7 Spiritual Laws of Success. Listening to them consistently will allow your cellular body to absorb them organically and they are values to live by, because they will set you free! Moreover, they are directly related to your acting career.

➢ Keep up your inner work, agreements with yourself, meditation, diet and exercise and most importantly remember to breathe deeply and slowly ALL the time. This work is not only important for your soul but also your Brand. I find it helpful to prepare a daily diary with a balance of all the elements in my day. At the end of the day, I feel I have been constructive and looked after every aspect: my body, my spirit, my craft, and my personal life.

➢ Sounds like a lot of work doesn't it? Think of it as a full time job doing what you love! You are working on yourself because you love yourself and your art, so all you need is to be disciplined with your time management. Balance is excellent because it will give you everything you desire.

Chapter 4

From Despair to Ecstasy

In the days following the fruits of my efforts to contact these two Production Companies, I focussed on learning the script for my audition with one of them. Meanwhile, my meeting with the other soon came up.

As the day of my meeting with the all-important casting director dawned, I was up and preparing for my trip to their office and ensuring I was going to be my best. I thought about what I would talk about with her and how I would ask for her advice and a casting. I was as nervous as hell. After my 'courier' escapade she was either going to love me or hate me.

As I entered her office, I took in the countless black and white photographs of actors on her walls. Her walls were covered with pictures. She invited me to sit down. As I sat down she launched into a tirade of abuse at my gall to presume that she would ever consider entertaining the thought of giving me a job over all the trained actors on her walls who were currently out of work and had paid their dues. She literally tore me to pieces. Turns out the answer to my question about my escapade was, she hated me.

As I walked out of her office I could hardly feel my legs or my body. I made it to my car before I broke down into the most uncontrollable sobs. I honestly thought that was the end of my career. I was absolutely devastated, in disbelief about how it could all have gone so wrong. I had never experienced such venom in my entire life. My sobbing continued for the better part of a week. I was inconsolable. How could my dream be dashed like that? Little did I know that years later I would have a guest role in the show that casting director worked for at the time. I had learnt a valuable lesson. Having the passion to go to all lengths was not enough. I had an opportunity to meet with a very influential person who could potentially employ me and I didn't do my research to find out how I needed to speak to her so that I could give myself the best possible opportunity. Further, had I known about self-referral then, I may not have allowed it to have such a destructive impact.

When I managed to pull myself together and resurface, it was time to focus on my casting with the other Production Company. In my mind, by the sheer ignorance I had about the industry, (there was no such thing as the Internet then), I really didn't know where to begin, I honestly thought this casting was my last chance to become an actor. Putting despair aside, I prepared as best I could. When the day arrived, I ensured I looked great and knew my script and got there in good time. To my absolute astonishment, I was greeted by a kind, tall, casting director, who was very nice to me. I was so nervous in my casting; I think I ran through my script in record speed. I was just grateful to get through it! I remember it was a Friday preceding a long weekend. He told me to give him a call after the long weekend to find out how it went.

That was the longest long weekend ever. As time ticked by, I became more and more hysterical, realising how high the stakes were for me. I was a mess. The following Tuesday I was up at the crack of dawn waiting for office hours to commence, so that I could make the call. By the time we spoke I was so anxious I broke down in tears. That's when this casting director realised just how much it meant to me. He invited me to a meeting.

When I arrived at the meeting he sat me down and said he had called me in because he saw something in me. That I definitely needed training but I had something. I HAD SOMETHING! I blurted out just how much it means to me and that I was prepared to put the work in and he proceeded to write down some directions for me to follow. Finally I had some advice from someone who knew the industry. I was so grateful.

That day I left his office with a list of instructions including agents and classes, an appointment with a reputable agent and a Mentor. I had gone from devastation to absolute elation. I was flying so high! From then on my career really began. However, I was lucky he was generous and kind to me. Putting myself through so much emotional stress was not good for my health.

Suggested Choices

- ➢ Your dream will propel you beyond your perceived limits.
- ➢ Inspiration is the best platform for Creativity. Imagine being in a state of inspiration all the time! If you follow my suggestions, you will enjoy inspiration!
- ➢ The danger lies in allowing it to take your entire existence over. As much as it can be positive, it can also blind you to making good choices, if it is not coming from the right place. In my case I was emotionally unhinged due to my anxiety and completely obsessed.
- ➢ If I had some awareness of whom I was when I met with the first Casting Director, the meeting may have upset me, but it would never have had the same devastating effect it had on me emotionally. A wiser choice would have been to see through this woman's anger to the substance of what she was telling me, which was not to quit, as I thought, but to train as an actor and pay my dues. An even wiser move would have been not to take it personally. That is something you will learn as you begin to practice self-referral.
- ➢ Self-development is very important. As we grow, our insecurities and we all have them, can prevent us from seeing the good in situations and take up valuable energy as we try to second guess people we perceive to be better than us. This is one area the Four Agreements come in handy.
- ➢ If you are able to find someone who can guide you, it will help you immensely. Especially, if as in my case it is someone who has a respected position in the industry. There is no harm in asking someone to become your mentor. These days, when people do a lot of mentoring, they can sometimes charge for their time. There is always someone who can help you further your education. In turn, you may be in a position to help someone else!
- ➢ Are we still breathing? Remember to Breathe, deeply and slowly all the time.

Chapter 5

So Excited!

As soon as I got home I just about gave my family a heart attack! They could not believe how happy I was! They really couldn't understand why it would mean so much. As far as they were concerned, I was going through a phase and I would grow out of it and get a real job. I was on top of the world.

I quickly got to work making calls to enrol into courses and I made my first appointment with an agent. I realised I had to make some money to do all this. I joined Promotions Agencies and started doing promotional work, which was flexible but somewhat unreliable. I also started working nights on the door at clubs, to keep my days free for castings as much as possible.

My life was a roller coaster, a very fast roller coaster. I was later described to be in a permanent state of anxiety. My friends used to say that I didn't need drugs I was already so high! Pretty soon I moved out of home. Travelling 30kms twice a day each way to and from home was taking its toll. I would perhaps do a promotion during the day, travel home, then travel back and work at night and travel home. My health kept suffering from pure stress. Moving out wasn't that easy either. All of a sudden I realised just how much I took for granted at home, the little things like a pair of scissors or having an iron. I was broke. Had I not been quite so impulsive, I may have prepared myself financially prior to jumping in the deep end. All my work was flexible, which is great for acting, but very unstable financially. Being in that situation is very stressful.

My social life was booming. Meeting people at promotions, at clubs and through acting meant a constant party. I dated people and I wanted to find love, but no one really registered in that speed. I had lots of fun doing unusual things like the motor show for ten days, ten hours a day, or golf tournaments, racing, launches, sailing and the list went on.

Do you see a theme emerging here? You may think it all sounds glamorous, but being on a roller coaster is being out of control. I was doing too much and my health was suffering. Acting became my life. There was no balance and the rest of my life suffered.

That is why I stress it is very important to sort out any issues or health problems you have and live a holistic life, without drama. I may have been lucky to start getting those acting jobs, but was I really giving my full attention to work when so much was going on and I was anxious? At the time of course I thought I was. But it is impossible to be fully present, as you need to be, when life is a drama. My lesson was to keep working on myself to conquer this imbalance.

When I met my first agent, I have to say it wasn't what I expected at all. In my imagination I pictured a glamorous office with lots of glossy photographs on the walls. A rather conservative and intimidating woman, who ushered me into an office, in her home, met me. I didn't know what to expect from this meeting. We just had a chat. Thanks to the recommendation of my Mentor, she agreed to represent me straight away. I couldn't believe it. I was so happy. The agency was obviously above board and the agent knew what she was talking about.

Then it was time to get to work. I arranged to meet the photographer to organise the photo shoot for my headshot and I made calls for courses, enrolling into Showbiz College soon after. I also started working with my first drama coach. The photographer was an older lady who took photos in alleyways and strange places. I still remember my first shots. She said I had so many expressions and that meant I would make a great actor. Naturally, I really liked her.

Soon after I joined the agency the castings started happening and I had to juggle work even more. I won the first casting I went for. My first job was an RTA Commercial. It was a night shoot in a nursery. It was very exciting. I was playing the girlfriend and I was being featured. The set looked beautiful and the costumes were great. I loved mine. It was a long night but I loved every minute of it. It was so great to be surrounded by professionals creating this story. But something did happen that night. I had a phobia and I was in the worst possible place for it, at night in a nursery full of lights. So although I was working, I was distracted by this very real fear. I had been working on this phobia with Reiki and hypnosis for some time but it didn't seem to be helping.

My agent was very happy I got the first job I went for. That was the beginning of my career. I was finally being submitted for good roles as I kept up with my training.

Suggested Choices

➢ When you have to do other work to supplement your income, I suggest you work smart. You can just as easily choose to wait on tables for instance, which pays very little and is physically exhausting, as you can choose to get into corporate role playing, learn the stock market, hosting, Teaching, writing, jobs that do not take your energy for Acting away and reward you. It is said that the harder people work the less they are paid. It is well worth your while to choose to WORK SMART not hard. It will free you to be the artist you wish to be. Having financial stability allows you to enjoy your craft as an Actor.

➢ Actors are required to do many things, hence the more skills you accumulate the better. It helps to have accents, sing, dance; it makes you "marketable". It is also advisable to have a drama coach to work with, if you are not able to study at one of the main drama schools and participate in short courses. It is always preferable to audition to enter credible drama schools, because they hold Graduation Days, when agents are invited, as well as casting directors. Actors are quite often chosen from these days, granted the opportunity to hit the ground running and avoid looking for an agent.

➢ Loving yourself is so important. Be gentle, forgiving, do your best and have Fun! After all, isn't that why we do what we do? A great exercise is to look in the mirror and thank yourself for who you are!

➢ Always remember to Breathe, slowly and deeply all the Time.

Chapter 6

A Working Actor

I will never forget my very first contract as an Actor. It was a play called "A Sporting Chance" with the Victorian Arts Centre and it was also set to tour Victoria, for high school students. I was in awe as I entered the Victorian Arts Centre. I felt like a serious Actor and I wanted to do my absolute best. It was an honour to be there and to be given this opportunity.

The role I was going for was a young girl called Nancy, who was the outcast, the one who didn't really fit in, but who set a goal and achieved it. I loved Nancy. She was so me! I did my audition and the director sat me down for a chat. She asked if I was afraid of heights, as I would have to deliver a monologue six feet above the ground. Of course I said NO, as memories of being stuck half way up Ayers Rock and not being able to move flooded my mind. I really wanted this job.

When my agent called to say I had won the role, I was ecstatic. I was also relieved not to have to juggle work to keep afloat. For a few months at least, the constant stress of juggling would be eliminated. I enjoyed the welcome feeling of security. Rehearsals were to begin the following Monday.

On the Sunday evening preceding rehearsals, I had an accident and dislocated my ankle. As I arrived to rehearsal on crutches, the company considered replacing me. My role was very physical and we would be doing two or three shows a day. I needed to get back on my feet if I wanted to keep my job. Some would say I sabotaged myself by putting myself out of action. I would agree, though of course it was subconscious. Our self-saboteurs are very sneaky, but they are vicious sometimes. That evening I had a Reiki session with a practitioner who prayed for a miracle.

The miracle happened. The very next day I was on my feet and off my crutches! As I travelled on the tram to and from work each day, I would thank God I was a full time working Actor. In my eagerness, I didn't care that I was badly bruised from climbing up and falling down rungs on something resembling a diving board every day. It was a while before they decided to put rubber on the rungs. I also didn't care that I felt so dizzy suspended above the ground delivering my monologue, because I was afraid of heights.

It was my first experience working with an ensemble of professional Actors. Being young and lacking confidence due to the fact I did not graduate from a drama school, despite the fact I took as many classes and worked as hard as I could, I felt quite intimidated. They seemed to be a breed of their own. I remember them complaining about small things and thinking how grateful I was.

They say, quite often, Art Imitates Life. Somehow, my role as the outsider translated itself to my experience of the ensemble. I am certain my own insecurities as a young Actor had a lot to do with that. It seemed, however to be an ongoing theme during the five month tour of the show.

Pretty soon our tour date arrived. I packed suitcases, hats, coats, everything I needed. It soon became apparent I would be responsible for carrying it all! I was less than overjoyed, as I had to trudge around with my luggage from motel to motel, holding the others up in the process. The first time we ordered drinks at the local country pub, I ordered a glass of champagne. The barman was visibly shocked. As the others played pool, I heard him say, in his ten years at the pub, no one had ever ordered champagne. He begrudgingly opened the bottle, then preceded to convince me to keep drinking, because he knew he could never get rid of it. I should tell you I am not a big drinker. I lived to regret that experience.

Touring is an experience in itself. When you tour, you either have yourself or the ensemble for company. Sometimes everyone wants to do the same things and sometimes they don't. I had never had to do things, like going to the movies, alone before. There were times when it became quite frustrating. There were also great times. We tried to make the best out of every place we visited and performed in. So we went to the Grampians and stayed in a B&B, stayed in a Motel called This'll Do Me in the middle of nowhere and hired a houseboat for a weekend. Horse riding didn't go very well for me. It was my first time and I was very nice to the horse, until it took off and threw me. I landed in hospital, with the doctor asking if I had an understudy. Of course, I didn't.

The show must go on. It did, and each time we went away after a short break, I ensured I packed less and less to carry on tour. It was on one day, travelling through the countryside, I had an inspiration. I envisioned meeting a prominent Producer from a Huge Production House. They were doing some great work, making big box office films. I wanted this person to remember me, so I decided to send a photograph for ten days with correspondence on the back of each photo, divided into pieces he would have to put together. I was so inspired and happy with my choice. It turns out, a while later, when I attended the AFI Awards and he had won an award, he recognised me. All he said was something to the effect of "I remember you!" and proceeded to introduce me to his peers. That was the result of all that hype and effort. I was unable to see them when I went to Sydney later.

The tour ended at the Victorian Arts Centre. That was the pinnacle of my experience of that show. I was so happy to have met the other actors. I felt sad when it ended. My lesson from that experience was that I did not have to suffer and injure myself to play that role. I deserved to be there just as much as the other actors. In fact Audiences related to my character because she was the Underdog.

Suggested Choices

> ➢ When you are in a meeting with a director, do not lie about skills. As in my case, those lies will come back and bite you! Be Authentic and trust that you will be appreciated for your own unique talent. Each of us has a unique talent. You will recognise your own when you feel excited about something you do.

> ➢ Regardless of your training, if you win a role, it is because you deserve it and you belong there.

> ➢ There is no need to suffer when you are playing a role, as in my case bruising myself and dislocating my ankle and falling off a horse. Believe it or not, self-sabotage is very common and subconscious, which means you are not aware of it. It is not until limiting beliefs are eliminated, that we can get out of our own way to success. To eliminate limiting beliefs NLP or Neuro Linguistic Programming is excellent. If I knew how to Love myself then, would I repeat bashing myself up?

> ➢ Everyone has their issues and Actors are no exception. In fact as Artists we are more sensitive than most. When you concern yourself with second-guessing other people's thoughts of you remember: Everyone ultimately cares about himself or herself more than they care about you! Other people's opinions are none of your business. This is where Self Referral comes in. If you become secure within yourself and operate from Spirit, you will never worry about anyone else. In fact, you will feel secure enough to go into service for others and people will genuinely connect with you. That is why The Four Agreements are so good to practise, as are the values in the 7 Spiritual Laws of Success.

> ➢ Touring is a great growing experience. When you tour with a show, you learn a lot about yourself. Whether you are in constant company or you are alone, you still experience a journey of discovery.

> ➢ With regard to my vision, I have always found it important to follow them; they have resulted in the completion of great projects. It is not uncommon for Actors to go to any

lengths to get work. It is important however, not to go too far, resulting in a lack of respect. It is a fine line sometimes. It can go either way. If you get to know yourself you will know whether its ego or spirit driving you and you will be best placed to use your discretion.

➤ Always remember to Breathe, deeply and slowly, all the time. Meditate every day. Why? Apart from obvious health and cognitive benefits, your creativity will sky rocket and you will place yourself in a state of self-referral! As you connect to your source, you become more and more inspired.

Chapter 7

Addicted to Drama

As an actor, I was fortunate to work quite often. I worked on commercials, some of which were fun and some of which were just hard work. I remember one commercial where we had to wait in a leaking garage on a wet and cold day for hours and froze.

On another commercial shoot for cheese, I played a bride, sitting on the hood of a vintage car and being fed pieces of cheese. It was a very artistic shot but it took six hours and I have never been able to eat that type of cheese again! Sometimes, it is not a glamorous profession.

I did a show called "New Balls Please" at La Mama Theatre, in a very intimate environment. It was theatre in the round. I worked with my drama coach who directed it and fellow actors, where we thrashed out a love triangle on a tennis court.

I also worked on a show called "Therapy", a rock musical, where I played Constance, a walking, singing, talking dictionary. On The Comedy Company I played Con the Fruiterer's daughter, Toula and then we appeared in the Moomba Parade in Melbourne. I am the original Toula! I worked on television making guest appearances on shows as well. It was all going so well.

Or so I thought. My career seemed to be taking off, but my anxiety was not exactly dissipating. I found it difficult to deal with and the more difficult I found it, the busier I made myself. I was running in all aspects of my life. It is said that most people wake up feeling like there is something wrong every single morning and that was my experience. I would find it hard to breathe and when I had an attack I would hyperventilate. Something usually upset me deeply before that happened. Past trauma was running a very strong program within me. Though I wasn't focussed on the past, my subconscious and my cellular body were.

Despite working quite regularly, I would spend extended periods waiting for the phone to ring. Actors are known to wait for calls from their agents. During those times I would get so sad and feel so helpless. It meant so much to me to be working. At times I went for roles I really wanted, like feature films for instance and the choice for the actor would come down to a couple of us. If I didn't win the role, having been so close, I would destroy myself with grief. I would drink and behave destructively because I was so disappointed. I took every rejection personally. There was no consoling me. My lesson was to keep myself creatively busy, so that I didn't wait by the phone and to learn not to take rejection so personally. Nothing was worth my wellbeing.

The impact of such emotional upheaval was monumental in my life. I found it difficult to juggle jobs and money. In my social life I was the organiser. Everyone used to call me to find out what was happening. In my personal life, I was disappointed often. I was always under the impression I would get married and live happily ever after, but that dream seemed to be the most unattainable. Even though I thought I wanted it so much, nothing would compare to Acting and Acting was what occupied my mind. My family life was challenging. My whole life was out of balance because I was so engrossed in acting. That meant that I wasn't really present and everything else just seemed to be a haze. I remember being aware of it, but I didn't know what I could do about it. I kept up my personal growth work.

I was on a ride I had no control over. My finances suffered because it was often difficult to juggle everything and all the work I did was unreliable. I was under a lot of stress, but I had no awareness of it. I was looking for love in all the wrong places; I was a mess. There are so many ways to perceive things. To the outsider I looked like a successful working actor with lots of friends, a great social life and many admirers. Inwardly, I was too delicate and too vulnerable to handle it all. On a couple of occasions I was given some amazing opportunities to cast for roles and I was too immature and too anxious to do my best. I missed those opportunities and I later regretted that. My lesson was to do my best with every opportunity.

It was clear that I needed to do more work on myself, to give myself the support I needed to succeed. As it happens, the Universe conspired in my favour.

Suggested Choices

> ➢ Preparation is everything. If you prepare for your audition, there is no room for error.

> ➢ Your Audition is YOUR TIME. Make the most of your time and take your time.

> ➢ Life Balance is paramount. Establish a working routine that best serves you in your career as an actor. It will give you the ability to enjoy every aspect of your life.

> ➢ Be Present when you work. If you practice meditation and Self Referral, as well as non-judgement, your mind chatter will dissipate and you will be able to be present and attentive. The benefit here is you will be able to listen to direction and respond in the best possible way.

> ➢ Never take an opportunity for granted. Every opportunity deserves respect and equal dedication to excellence. Every job is your biggest job. My agent used to say, "there are no small parts, only small actors". So many times I have seen actors drunk or lazy or apathetic before an audition. A little secret: Gratitude will always bestow you with more of what you love! My advice is to be thankful and take responsibility to ensure you do your best, as per the 4 agreements!

> ➢ REJECTION IS NOT PERSONAL. There are so many variables and stakeholders involved in making decisions to cast Actors. It can come down to something minute. If you ensure you always do your best, taking it personally will only be destructive to you.

> ➢ Don't take it out on yourself. It's not your fault if you did your best. As Dr Wayne Dyer would say, there is always a reason for everything that happens and it only means something better will come along! I am paraphrasing here. Dr Dyer's Ah and Om meditations are excellent for creativity and gratitude!

> ➢ Learn to move on. As soon as you do an audition, forget it. It saves waiting for the phone to ring and putting your life on hold. This is the power of detachment. Let it go, move to the present and that will make you happy. Detachment is a lesson in the Buddhist Philosophy. I studied Buddhism and

learnt the value of compassion and service, two of the most beneficial lessons of my life. It helped heal relationships and connect me with people in a very real way. Do you think that may benefit your Creativity and career?

> Trust that you will attract exactly what you create and what is perfect for you. There is no need to worry about a thing. All you need to do is be aware of what you are thinking. Soon you will realise your thoughts create your reality.

> You are your attention; begin to think about where you place your attention. That will create your reality.

> Remember to Breathe, slowly, deeply and all the time.

Chapter 8

Sydney here I come!

I was always enamoured by Sydney. I had travelled there on a couple of occasions for acting work. It was on one of those occasions I met a casting director who, upon meeting me, picked the telephone up and called an agent to represent me. This agent was based in Melbourne and Sydney. I subsequently left my first agent upon this casting director's recommendation.

The way it happened was quite fortuitous. I was moving out of my place in Melbourne and a friend in the agency told me she was going to Sydney for a month and asked if I would like to join her. A house had been offered to us to stay. Without a thought I said yes. I had a feeling I would be staying in Sydney for a little longer than a month, so I decided to wrap things up in Melbourne. I still remember my family when I told them. They were shocked and disappointed. They didn't want me to go. But just as I left my mother and ran off in primary school on my very first day, I decided to leave Melbourne. I arranged going away parties and said goodbye to my friends.

I was so excited by my decision I really didn't think twice. I remember my poor family at the airport and my little sister so sad I was leaving. As soon as I landed in Sydney, my journey of self-discovery truly began. As it turned out my friend was delayed and would not be arriving for two weeks, so I secured accommodation for that time. On the way to my destination, the cab broke down on Oxford Street. In a panic I called the house and luckily they said they were very close by, so they came to my rescue. Soon after I walked into a two-storey terrace house in Paddington, ready to stay with a couple.

The couple were very nice, the girl even more so. The next problem presented itself. The house was infested with cockroaches. They were everywhere! I had never seen cockroaches before and as I have a phobia I found myself in a nightmare. As the others didn't seem to be too bothered I didn't want to make a scene. I kept telling myself it would only be two weeks until my friend arrived. I will never forget the first night there and every night subsequent to that, as I couldn't sleep. I kept jumping up thinking cockroaches were crawling over me. I was petrified.

Even more petrifying was the fact the girl was a bisexual and took a liking to me. I was a naïve Melbourne girl who thought she was being very hospitable and friendly taking me shopping and showing me around, until she made a pass at me. Then my nightmare doubled in intensity and I spent my time between avoiding cockroaches and avoiding her.

The drama kept coming. At the time I was supposed to meet my friend and move into the house that had been offered to us, the house fell through and I was supposed to be moving that day. All of a sudden I was forced to find a place to stay in a day. The adventure began. I called on one of two people I knew in Sydney and we drove to the north shore to meet my friend. Then we drove around to find a place to stay. I ended up in a type of boarding house in Elizabeth Bay, but not before a lot of trudging around in a downpour of rain. It was the most torrential weekend Sydney had seen in years.

In the first six months I moved seven times. So many things happened. I was robbed, I moved in with another couple and it didn't work out, then I moved in with my boyfriend and that didn't work out, so I stayed with a friend until I found a place. The good thing was although I barely knew two people in Sydney when I arrived; pretty soon I knew lots of people. I made friends with models, actors, directors, filmmakers and photographers. I fell into the right crowd, so to speak, thanks to my boyfriend who was an artist.

Although I went through some tough times, it didn't occur to me to return to Melbourne. I simply solved every situation as it came up. When the chips were down I just became more resourceful. It was such a novelty being in a new city and being able to run around Oxford Street in orange cut off shorts, without anyone blinking an eye. It was a really fun time. I was going out with my boyfriend, we had great friends and lots of events to go to, a great social life. I was very keen to start pursuing my career. I discovered I was a survivor and the Universe protected me. In all that instability I was learning that that even though I was but a leaf in the wind, I was looked after.

On Location, Bondi cliffs for She Saw The Seesaw

Suggested Choices

➢ When you prepare to make a move as big as moving cities, it is well worth preparing for it, by checking finances, accommodation, ensuring there is work for you and looking after your affairs. It is looking after you!

➢ As 'shit' happens, it's always good to have a plan B. Of course all my plans were laid out but things do fall through. It is not what happens but how we react to it that matters. I was lucky I was attuned to finding solutions to problems rather than dwelling on the whys and how's. We cannot control people, places or things. The only thing we can control is how we react to circumstances.

➢ When things go 'wrong', it is so easy to fall into traps like thinking about the reason something happened, or feeling sorry for ourselves "why me?" or worse feeling defeated "oh well, I tried and it didn't work". When things happen to challenge us, its time to grow more resourceful. If you see the solution and not the problem, you have an opportunity for expansion and a world of possibility.

➢ Remember breathe slowly, deeply all the time. Listen to the 7 Spiritual Laws, practice the 4 agreements, meditate, exercise and eat well. What you eat will express itself in who you are and what you think of yourself. As a Brand, you may think of yourself as an athlete, you must be at the top of your game.

Chapter 9

Getting Down To Business

Soon I found somewhere to live and settled in. As my life seemed to settle, my relationship broke down. It was a really dark time. All of a sudden my casual work dried up and I struggled. Regardless, I would walk half an hour to my two-hour dance class and read Madonna's biography for inspiration. As I looked for work to make a living, I started my career in Sydney.

I started working with a coach at the Actor's Space. That journey lasted for three years, doing workshops with other actors and developing a play together. It was a very collaborative process as well as a bonding experience. We did some great work together, not without the occasional drama of course! Those three years were an era of creativity and fostering of relationships. Of course I continued my training, doing on camera workshops, American Accent classes, Shakespeare classes with esteemed directors, my absolute favourite with the esteemed Rowena Balos. My time at the Actor's Space became a lifestyle as much as a learning experience.

During that time I continued my self-development journey by doing lots of courses and reading and research. I was fascinated by personal growth, probably more to help ease my own suffering, but also from the point of view of an actor and observation of human behaviour. I delved into psychology and discovered therapy.

My time at the Actor's space rewarded me with some great friends. I moved in with one friend, another chapter. We had some great times together and collaborated creatively on projects. It was at that time I made my first short film. The organiser of Tropfest, John Polson once spoke to me on the phone as I was working on someone else's film and suggested I make my own film. That seemed to be all I needed to hear.

Before I knew it, I was in pre-production for my first short epic, with a cast of thousands, several locations and four days of shooting. It was a producer's nightmare on a tiny budget. Seeing as I was the co producer, along with my friend, the onus fell on me. I arranged cast, crew, locations, transport, catering, equipment, hair and makeup, everything we needed in record time and with little cost. The great thing at that time was that so many people were making films, we all helped each other. Getting an entire production together in such a short time was no easy feat, but once I set my sites on something, no obstacle could possibly deter me.

I wrote a film about a girl from two different perspectives, being a victim and being empowered. It was called "She Saw the See-Saw'. The film was completed after quite a few challenges with logistics, which wore my nerves thin. By the end I was exhausted, especially as I also played the heroine. It was longer than the required limit, but because the organiser knew my story I had my first short film screen at the Tropfest Short Film Festival as a finalist!

Suddenly I was sitting in front of a big screen as an audience member and my film started screening. I was really embarrassed! It was very personal putting my work up there for all to see. When the feedback started pouring in from people, I avoided the attention. That was an experience I won't forget. I imagine many artists would feel a little exposed putting their work up for the world to judge. Now I was also hooked on making films.

The Three Amigos

Suggested Choices

➢ Obstacles will inevitably come up. Do not let obstacles stand in the way of your success. Why let a little obstacle stop you from achieving your goal? Obstacles are simply challenges to master. Keep your dream alive and focus on that. Every obstacle is an opportunity for expansion it's Awesome!

➢ If you follow your creative dreams your soul will thank you. A very easy way to establish if you are on your soul path is to do a feelings check: if you feel good, you may be assured you are on the right track.

➢ The ideal situation is to be well prepared. In some situations however that is not always possible. You can choose to throw yourself in the deep end or take baby steps. Some people work best under pressure and some don't.

➢ Always remember to breathe and look after yourself. That is an expression of love! As you read this book, practice breathing this way and make it a habit. Breathing air into your body opens you up to life in full and all that is.

➢ When you are producing and something doesn't go to plan, as is often the case, especially in low budget productions, don't panic. The greatest skill a producer offers is the ability to solve problems calmly and efficiently.

➢ Practicing meditation, the Four Agreements and the 7 Spiritual Laws of Success will directly benefit your work and give you creative freedom and peace of mind.

On set She Saw the Seesaw, last day of the Shoot

On the Set of She Saw the Seesaw. Here we are in King's Cross on day 1 of a four-day shoot. Operating on a tiny budget meant we had a minimal crew. Those days it didn't even occur to us to gain a permit to shoot, everyone was making short films!

Chapter 10

Growing Up

Juggling casual work finally came to a halt when I found work in a call centre. No longer did I have to worry about where my next dollar was coming from whilst I pursued my career. At last I had flexible work that was regular and dependable. It was such a great environment, filled with actors, directors, musicians who understood the necessity for flexibility. We all covered for each other when we had other work. It was also great because we could exchange information about the industry and work, so we always knew when there was a production coming up. We became friends and followed each other's careers, going to shows and seeing bands perform. It was a great lifestyle.

As my soul journey continued I delved further into different healing modalities. I did inner child workshops and re-birthing, found meditation, sought out different courses and spirituality. I was a huge advocate for therapy. I completed courses in relationships, conflict resolution, and emotional intelligence, whilst attending seminars that inspired and empowered people. I also studied Buddhist meditation.

Meanwhile my friends were getting into some bad habits and life became complicated for a while. I found myself trying to rescue my brilliantly talented and creative friends, before I fell into the pond and joined them for five minutes of my life. I discovered very quickly that my delicate nature could not possibly survive that lifestyle. Everyone I knew seemed to be living the life of excess. The relationships I formed seemed to follow the same pattern. Where there was excess there was trouble. One of my friends paid dearly with his life.

I tried to find balance and peace in my life. I was a spiritual being but I was also susceptible to that exciting lifestyle, which seemed to surround me. Although I wanted to find true love, love was the last thing I encountered. I had to let my circle of friends go and create the space for healthy relationships to come in. That was the loneliest time of my life. Whilst they were partying, I was left sad and alone. But I had to stay true to myself and not fall into what was popular. I had to tell myself that in creating a space, I would meet like-minded people, with a healthy attitude to life.

It wasn't as simple as that. Although I tried to create a holistic life I continued to be surrounded by temptation at every front. It was part and parcel of the industry I was in. In my experience, creative people are often so fragile and open to all that is. That is a great quality and a potentially dangerous one.

I was obsessed with acting and making films. I always envisioned my creative projects before they came to life. I was growing and life imitated art. I was a child in wonder. I loved nature and the sun and the sea and the universe. I was in the zone. Life finally started making sense.

Suggested Choices

> ➤ The reason I emphasise The Toltec Path to Freedom and the 4 Agreements, as well as Dr Deepak Chopra's 7 Spiritual Laws of Success so much to you, is so that you can practise Self-Referral. Apart from the benefit it will have on your career, it will benefit you immensely as a person. If you have Self-Referral, you keep your own power and you will not feel the need to compromise yourself as I did.

> ➤ Know that, although you may see loved ones fall into traps and feel the need to help them, they are responsible for their own journey. By helping them in their weakness, you propagate the weakness. By trusting in their success and allowing them to achieve it, you are able to assist in it. There is a wonderful chapter in "The Vortex" by Esther and Jerry Hicks about relationships.

> ➤ Remember to breathe deeply and slowly and listen to your body as choices emerge. Your body will tell you if something feels right or not. The more in tune you become, the louder the guidance will be for you.

> ➤ It is difficult to achieve creative inspiration surrounded by toxicity. You are your attention. If you place your attention on what gives you joy, you will never lose your way.

> ➤ Work Smart. Its so stressful trying to make ends meet whilst you are doing courses and running to castings and juggling acting work with regular work. Find something that suits your career and pays well.

> ➤ Networking is Very Important. When you network you make friends and friends normally prefer to work with friends. Not only that, you have your ear to the ground and know exactly what is happening and what you can pursue with your agent. You can think of networking as placing yourself in situations where you will naturally meet people on the same path.

> ➤ One of the most important ingredients is the value of friendship and surrounding yourself with like-minded people, sharing your spirit for creativity. The support,

encouragement, positivity and community Actors and Artists create together, are some of the richest gifts in life.

➢ Pitfalls! Creative People can have some unhealthy habits. Find what is healthy for you. You can participate on your own terms. Put yourself and your needs first. Surround yourself with high vibration people, so that you all benefit each other. By now, you know how to follow a healthy blueprint.

➢ If you are working on a creative project, getting a group of people each with their own unique talent to contribute is very important and very constructive, not to mention fun!

➢ Be a work in progress. I still say I am a work in progress I love that. Keep growing and learning. There is a saying that goes something like, when you stop learning you die!

➢ If you do falter, please forgive yourself. Beating yourself up will not help you as much as being aware of your actions and rectifying them. Believe in your success, no one can love and support you better than you.

Chapter 11

My Biggest Project Yet

I focussed on balance and I felt that, although Acting was still so important to me as a career, I was exploring other aspects of life. I paid more attention to personal relationships, my other work and my social life. Although everything seemed to be the same, my awareness had shifted. My spiritual work and personal growth continued. I made new discoveries and kept trying to improve myself. I always did my best. I didn't know exactly why, but it seemed to be a driving force in my life.

When inspiration struck, all I could see was the end goal. I faced major challenges, but I overcame them. When I decided to make my short films, I had a vision, the story and the script practically wrote themselves and I simply found the means to make them. That may sound simple, but it meant casting for actors, sourcing locations and permission to shoot there, recruiting crews, arranging everything from equipment to catering, make up and hair, all within tiny budgets that needed to be sourced.

When I had a creative vision, the story had a life of its own. The most rewarding of all aspects of film-making is watching a story unfold.

I hadn't had a creative vision for a couple of years. At this point I will confess if you haven't already guessed I was quite a self-involved actor, which is not uncommon in the Entertainment Industry.

It follows, then, that when I had this particular creative vision, I was astounded. In its simplest form, a wave of wealth encompassed the entire world, equalling resources globally, even though from a literal perspective it appeared as a world tsunami. My vision was powerful and the meaning so clear, that in my flu delirium, I took stock. I thought why couldn't we do that? Does poverty need to exist? I will remind you this came from a self involved Actor! I suddenly became passionate about creating a solution for world poverty.

As ideas go, I could have let something as ambitious and deluded as that slide. There was only one little problem. Instead of peacefully falling asleep at night, ideas would race in. It was like a radio in my head and before you think it, no I am not a schizophrenic. It was a creative flow that felt like an endless tap in my brain. Instead of sleeping, I started writing. I felt I was receiving divine guidance. There was no other way I could explain what was happening, because the ideas were foreign to me. No one was more surprised than me.

I was so involved in the idea I started talking to people about it. To my surprise, everyone relevant to the project was immediately attracted to it. Apparently they didn't think I was crazy. Before I knew it, I had a team enrolled in the project. It included a reporter/producer, a human rights expert, an environment consultant, a project manager and someone who specialised in charity. We started meeting every week. Others with relevant experience joined the cause. We established our team and a Committee of Advisors.

Very soon it was realised that my vision was actually synonymous with the Millennium Development Goals, which were part of the United Nations Millennium Project, headed by esteemed Economist Jeffrey Sachs. That heralded the beginning of a journey spanning over the last decade.

During the first year I went to auditions and worked as an actor, worked casually and headed the project, which was to empower not only those in developing nations, but all those who participated. The ideas were still keeping me up at night; I was immersed in Project Elevation and totally dedicated to the Millennium Project. After over a year of insomnia and working the equivalent of two full time jobs, I simply collapsed.

Suggested Choices

> Being in a state of inspiration is something we aspire to do as much as possible. As I learnt the hard way, it is imperative balance is adhered to. It is essential you keep to your holistic balanced lifestyle and learn how to 'switch off' in a healthy way. Focus on relationship, meditation, leisure-time; elements like these are imperative to your wellbeing.

> Pay respect to your body as much as your spirit. You will learn to listen to your body when your spirit wants to do more than you are humanly able to.

> As you practice meditation and become more aware of the Source you stem from and the unseen team supporting you, you may encounter your guides. It was my guides who provided those ideas in such a fashion. You can actually ask your guides to give you a break and begin again at a time that suits you!

> If you have a problem, you can hand it over to be taken care of. We may often think we demand a lot from God or the Universe, but in fact we do not demand enough and we also need to be specific about time. These themes may be unfamiliar to you now, but as you develop you will become more attuned.

Chapter 12

The Big Showdown

The first sign was forgetfulness. It was the most frightening experience I had ever had. I would get into my car to go to work, taking the same route I had taken for years and I would forget the way. I would come out of the elevator or bathroom at work and forget which way to go. It was too embarrassing to talk about, hence I didn't. In work I would be meticulous and in running the project I was, if anything over efficient, because I feared my brain letting me down at such a crucial time.

What followed was a collapse. My entire body shut down completely. I became very sick for twelve weeks and doctors couldn't tell me what was wrong. Antibiotics didn't work and my iron and white blood cells were so low I could not even walk. All my organs were shutting down.

Twelve weeks later I felt better and raced back to work! I was so bored with my own company; as usual I went hell for leather. A couple of months into work I collapsed again. I was diagnosed with Chronic Fatigue Syndrome, or CFS. My family brought me back to Melbourne. I had to abandon everything, which was anathema to me. I was very depressed.

I was bedridden again, this time for months. Managing one task per day was a major achievement. Can you imagine what that must be like? I started researching and finding help wherever I could. It was the darkest time of my life I had to do something.

I found out about CFS. I discovered long term stress and doing too much for extended periods can bring CFS on. It was common amongst elite athletes and people who drove themselves to their limits. Whilst many people can work a hundred hours a week, some people reach boiling point and collapse with this syndrome. While many people recharge their batteries when they sleep and feel refreshed in the morning, CFS sufferers never recharge their batteries and have flat batteries to run on. That is the simplest analogy I can give you. Of course it is a more complicated than that.

Despite my illness, my project was foremost on my mind. My family would berate me about wanting to solve world poverty when I was so ill. They kept telling me I needed to be well first. And I did. The lesson I was being taught was to slow down and pace myself. I was not allowed to work for a minimum of two years, but I couldn't stop thinking about Project Elevation.

I didn't fully learn the lesson, to pace myself. I would still go crazy when I felt better, because it is the most, boring illness and then I would crash, so I could have one or two good days and be out of action for a week or two. Another impact this illness had was to isolate me. It took me out of the rat race and placed me alone in recovery.

My creative juices kept flowing and I went back to Sydney and Project Elevation. My team had since gone onto other things. I decided I needed to collaborate with a Production Company to produce this series. Both the UNMP and Make Poverty History advised us "They were in competition". My response was, where is the competition if we are working toward the greater good?

Approaching Production Companies was a process that didn't bear fruit for some time. It was whilst I spoke with the Film and TV Office that someone suggested the CEO of a comparatively new Television Production Company doing extremely well and producing much Television Content called Freehand Television. Of course I simply picked up the phone and called them.

When this particular CEO's Personal Assistant called to set up a meeting, I couldn't believe it. I had gone through leading a team, to becoming ill and having to put the project on hold, to losing my team as a result, to losing The UNMP to which we had dedicated the whole project and my resources, to being rejected by Television Production Companies, to doubt and self examination, to rejection from Make Poverty History, because they were apparently in Competition too, to simply holding onto the vision and going forward and finally to this Meeting with the CEO of a very successful Television Production Company, Freehand Television!

As the time of the meeting approached, I was quite beside myself. I was extremely organised, on time and ready to fire. I found confidence I didn't know I had, however, what I realised in hindsight, was that it was my pure motivation to empower and inspire people that drove me. I achieved my intention.

When we were led into the meeting and exchanged business cards, the CEO expressed surprise at my ability to gain a meeting with him. My project resembled one they had in development. It was later that comment registered, as I de briefed with my friend. All I remember is my enthusiasm and pure passion driving the meeting and the conviction that this project would become a reality, even when I was told it was a 7 million dollar proposition and it had never been done before, which apparently, is not a good thing.

The original idea was of global proportion. It involved sending teams to the corners of the earth. As life would have it, I made a decision to move back to Melbourne. I took some time to settle, networking from scratch and making contact with all the casting directors, directors, sound studios I could to start working.

Freehand Television continued to mentor me to no avail, as the project was still not commercially viable. Until the inspiration came; it was so simple I didn't know why I hadn't considered it before. Instead of sending a number of teams to bring back stories, I would simply go out there and bring the stories back myself! I started writing again. The result was the creation of THE CRAZY CRUSADER.

The project has since had many reincarnations. Today it is a Facebook Page called The Crazy Crusaders, focussing on sustainable, humane, community driven solutions for our future outside the square we live in. The square is the dis-functional system we currently live in. It is a community on Facebook and now a TV segment in the Pilot for a new show! The genuine encouragement, support and help I have had from Freehand Television has not only filled me with gratitude. It has also inspired me to write other concepts for television programs.

As I learnt to pace myself, my health gradually improved. The gift of having so much time alone was becoming very clear to me. It was giving me the space to be creative and dwell in my imagination. That has been the most monumental gift of having CFS. It has allowed me to be more of who I really am at my core, a creative soul. It has also taught me to learn to actively love myself.

Sharing my ten-year battle with CFS was no easy feat. I experienced loss of income and savings, five years of attempting various natural healing modalities and finally medication, which to this day is keeping me upright! I am currently changing my body blueprint. I have been practicing Kelly Howell's guided healing meditations and have already achieved success with a couple of health issues.

My motivation in sharing my story with you is so that you can really feel the impact of my choices as well as the potential impact of the choices you make in your journey as an artist. My wish for you is to be inspired to lead a holistic life connected to your divine source. It is possible that you can be in a frequent state of inspiration if you establish the suggestions I have made for your inner life a daily practice.

It is important to realise we make choices every second. Some things are second nature and we don't perceive them as a choice. Everything is a choice. The more aware we become of the choices we are constantly making, the more we can benefit others and ourselves.

What we refuse others, we refuse ourselves; as you organically absorb the material I recommend for you, you will experience a connection not only with other people but everything around you. I started having a profound experience as I took my daily walk along the cliffs by the sea. When I started feeling connected, it was as if nature was talking to me. I was filled with elation and I would look around and see others doing their daily walk or run, on their mobile phones or headphones on and I could not believe they were missing it!

Chapter 13

Going to Castings

Whilst most people may decide to change career paths or jobs a few times in their lifetime and opt instead for perceived security and stable employment, actors go through thousands of castings in the course of their career, hence my emphasis on Self Referral, which eliminates feelings of rejection. Acting has been referred to as character building and it really is. One has to learn to deal with rejection without taking it personally. Sometimes it can come down to a look or the length of someone's hair. You just never really know and cannot know, so why worry?

Castings can be a mind field. I have heard so many actors say they dread auditions. As actors we are excited when we receive word we have a casting, because it is an opportunity to work at what we love best. Generally speaking, we place a lot of importance on castings because quite often they are for work we really want to do. Another element may be the financial reward, which may be substantial. The job may also raise an actor's profile and lead to more work.

We are faced with competition to win one acting job. So we have to deal with high expectations, high stakes and of course the fact that when we go for work, there are a few decision makers involved, who have to agree on one actor. If you do a casting for a commercial you have the casting director, the director(s), the producers, the client and the advertising agency, all coming together on a project. That is why I stress the importance of doing inner work as the difference between being a victim to external circumstances and rising above them and thriving. In fact, competition doesn't really exist! There is more than enough out there for everyone.

Over the years I have come up with my own winning formula for successful castings. Coming up, you will learn how to love, versus dread auditions with a simple click in perception!

Chapter 14

Successful Castings

Here are some simple tips for preparation:

1. When you receive details of the casting, work out the logistics, by mapping out your trip there and working out where you will park, how much it will cost etc. so that you are not stressed out or left out of pocket or left unprepared.
2. Rehearse, rehearse, and rehearse! Know your audition piece! Be fully prepared.
3. Estimate the time it will take to get there and allow plenty of time.
4. Pick out your wardrobe to fit the character you are playing.
5. Do your hair and makeup according to your character.
6. If you don't have a script, work from the brief, rehearse your reactions, expressions or actions. This is your Award winning Performance, not an Audition. More on that later!
7. Use your Secret Weapon. There is a chapter dedicated to your secret weapon to come, but here's a snippet specifically relevant to auditions: Put yourself in a

meditative state and imagine yourself getting there easily and effortlessly, being present and calm, imagine meeting the director and connecting, then playing the scene and receiving great feedback. You can imagine everything up to receiving your cheque and being grateful. Feel you already have the job. See yourself being filled with gratitude when you receive your cheque. Gratitude is so important, because it will bring you more of that which you love.

8. When the time comes to travel to your casting, state your intention to do a great job and win the acting role. Intention setting is coming up!

9. When you are in your casting, take your time to listen and understand direction and perform as if you have already won the role. Do not treat it like a rehearsal; imagine you are actually on set or stage or location, doing this job. Remember your audition time is just that, your time.

10. Always do your best and go in character. Be present and listen. That allows you to respond with authenticity. If you are practicing your 4 agreements (Don Miguel Ruiz) you will already do that.

11. One of the biggest pitfalls actors generally face is 'getting psyched out', which impacts on their performance. Things like other actors sitting in the waiting room that you consider to be more popular, have a higher profile, be more talented in your opinion, the casting director or director not giving you the response you are looking for, stumbling on lines and freezing, these are just some examples. If you are in Self-Referral none of this will matter. You will see everyone and everything as an extension of yourself rather than perceiving others in terms of higher or lower status. Can you see how doing the inner work I recommend for you would free you?

12. Luckily you are practicing Your Secret Weapon. By arriving in good time, just fifteen minutes before your audition, you can rest assured you will not run into the 'competition' too much, unless the casting runs late.

You can trust your secret weapon. You have already done the work!

13. Most of all HAVE FUN!

14. Remember: People usually buy you in the first few seconds. You don't have to let that pressure you. If you do your best, you may rest assured and let it go.

15. Always come back to the breath. Breathe slowly and deeply, in and out.

16. Never make excuses in an Audition, like the car accident you had, the flu you have etc. They are not interested in your problems. Leave your personal issues at the front door. We all have them. Simply do your best. As we say in Showbiz, the Show Must go On!

17. You are free to enjoy your Performance. Even if it is the only time you play this role, reap the reward of performing it and be grateful for the opportunity to do so. If you are practicing your Secret Weapon, you will feel secure that all is as it should be.

Chapter 15

Film

My experience of Film ranges from making and assisting in short films to performing in feature films. Quite often actors are approached to participate in non-budget productions. We do that for several reasons. If the filmmaker is an up and coming director/producer it's a great way to begin a working relationship. The film may be submitted to high profile short film festivals and provide a wide audience. Or performing in a great scene can provide the opportunity to put something great on our show reel. Regardless of the budget, it is always important to be professional.

It is common to fulfil many roles when you are working with limited budgets. For example my second short film was called PARTY POOP. It was a decadent romp in a yacht. I financed it myself and was able to pull together a great crew, a yacht, a location and the actors on a tiny budget. This film was relatively simple, just one location. I played the heroine, wrote and produced it.

Sometimes things don't go according to plan when working on low or no budget films. When I made TILL DEATH DO US PART, I wrote the script based on a real life story of an exotic dancer who was getting married. A friend read the script and loved and wanted to finance and direct it. I happily agreed. We went into pre-production. I arranged to have a suite at the Gazebo Hotel in Sydney and cast the actors, who were happy to participate in that particular genre, featuring gangsters, strippers and the like. As pre-production neared completion, in fact two days prior to the shoot, my friend pulled out with the funding. In two days I had raised the funding from the Eros Foundation, who loved the idea that my story humanised the sex industry.

When you create your own work, you have the opportunity to establish and market your Brand. TOUCH UPS WITH TULA is a character I developed and wanted to shop around. The first episode featured Actor Graham Harvey as a guest. Later I made 5 more episodes, now on You Tube, accosting celebrities like Tottie Goldsmith, Rob Morgan, Fiona Scott Norman, John Beland and Kevin Grise, with my Stylists to the Stars, Magic Mike and Bronny, touching them up and finding out all the nitty gritty! Very politically incorrect.

Feature films are very different. For one, they usually have a budget, which means one is not obliged to fulfil numerous roles in the production. If feature films have adequate distribution, they may propel your career to the highest possible standards. Most actors covet work in feature films. Professionalism as well as all the tools I have shared with you, like practicing Dr Deepak Chopra's 7 Spiritual Laws of Success for instance, will hold you in good stead, because they will bestow you with values that will endear you to others and attract more of the work you love to you.

In THE SEVENTH FLOOR, I was cast as Brooke Shield's assistant in an advertising firm. I remember the casting, I was anxious as I waited for two hours to go in, knowing the dire consequences when I arrived at work late. I remember going in to my casting after waiting so long and saying to the director:" I only have a few lines, what do you want me to do with them?" When I think back now, that was so arrogant! But luckily he laughed and I ended up with the role. It was the most high profile film and role I had ever played. Just being in the same room with two international stars and reading the script was amazing. Unfortunately, a lot of my work ended up on the cutting room floor, but not before I struck up a brief friendship with Brooke. It was so lovely to spend time with her. Whenever I have met incredibly successful people, the qualities that stand out are their humility and generosity. Values are such an integral part of fulfilling our full potential as humans on this planet.

In all I performed and or assisted in close to thirty films over the years. THE VENUS FACTORY or MONEY SHOT as it was later called was yet another experience. I was faced with playing a porn starlet. Another memorable role was one of a divorced mother, in KEEPING KIDS IN MIND, a harrowing character I dove into with great feedback from the Director.

I hope that these examples give you a glimpse into the world of film. The work is so rewarding. In film one has the opportunity to work with excellent scripts and stretch as an actor. You also have the opportunity to work with some (other) 'A' list actors. 'A' list actors are usually celebrities you find working all the time. There is an opportunity there of fostering relationships and learning more about our craft. Given that films usually take a few weeks in production, a strong camaraderie is often established, so by the time the wrap party happens, it is a huge celebration as well as a feeling of achievement for all involved.

Touch Ups with Tula, interview with John Beland

Wrap Party with Brooke Shields for "The Seventh Floor"

Suggested Choices

- ➢ You can source low or no budget films from Film Schools and other avenues like the Internet. I recommend doing some short films to add to your show-reel when you start your career.
- ➢ When you agree to participate in a non-budget film ensure you are doing it for the right reasons. Always make strategic decisions about your career. It is good to discuss these decisions with your agent if you have one. If not, working with emerging directors and producers may lead to future work and if the film you are working on is screened at prominent film festivals, it can also promote your career.
- ➢ If you decide to make films enlist people who possess skills you do not have. Create a Talent Bank. A talent bank is a group of individuals possessing a variety of skills relevant to your project. The other option is to go to film school and learn the technical side of making films.
- ➢ Helping other filmmakers is always good for future work. Creative projects are great to work on and one day they may help you too. It aligns with spiritual law.
- ➢ When you are on set be professional. Follow direction and listen to instruction. You may socialise when there is a break.
- ➢ Always remember to keep breathing, deeply and slowly, as it will place you in good stead, keep you grounded and able to deal with situations in a healthy way as they come up. If you are practicing the 4 Agreements, listening to The 7 Spiritual Laws of Success often, generally following the holistic blueprint I have described to you, you will be in a pure state of creativity and inspiration!

Chapter 16

Television

Television is a fast paced environment, where budgets and schedules are paramount. There are so many people involved in making television that it makes for a very fragile domino effect when anything goes wrong. It is the job of the producer and production team to ensure each production, sometimes like a little factory, keeps ticking to deliver projects on time.

As Actors, we are asked to arrive on time, go to make up and wardrobe and perform our best work in the least number of takes, so that we don't hold up the production. It is imperative we are well prepared and have the character and our lines down pat. Once again it is important for us to be Professional. Television directors don't always direct performance, in fact they rarely do. They generally advise you when your choice doesn't match their expectation of the scene. It is then they may offer you a different choice to make as an Actor. If you are practicing Self-Referral, you will be able to work well with a director.

Although most Actors dream of having a long standing contract on a show, a lot of actors make guest appearances. There is a small number of Actors who are banked on to be regular characters, by the networks. Of course as Actors, we aim to become one of those choices for the networks, although one actor I know has been contracted to a soap for the last twenty years and that may not be ideal for some. Putting your Secret Weapon into practice ensures that the sky is the limit for you, if Television is where you would like to be.

My experience in Television thus far, has been making guest appearances. Most recently I was seen hosting a TV Show and presenting on morning shows on Networks 7,9,10 as well as TVSN, here in Australia. I now love presenting! In fact I have been presenting my own segment in the Pilot of a new TV show.

It is always fun to participate in any production. To be surrounded by that world of creating drama or comedy and all it entails. Sometimes we don't receive the script for the next day until the evening before the shoot. Also, coming into any show as a guest, there is an aspect of fitting in to the environment, with the resident actors. Here your values will help connect you to your environment in an authentic way. Sometimes resident actors become bored and can focus on guest actors for fun. Generally Actors work very well together. Working with high profile directors is always great, as it may lead to future work. For instance in ME AND MY MONSTERS, I worked with a Director from the U.K Show "Vicar of Dibley". Nothing transcends the work. A good script and a 'juicy' character is our dream!

On the set Police Rescue, with Steve Bastoni

Suggested Choices

> ➤ Arrive on location on time. In this industry if you are late you tend not to work! Ensure you calculate your travel time and research the means to your destination, if that is not something that has already been arranged between your agent and the production manager. Use your Intention Setting, something I will explain to you in more detail as you read on.
> ➤ Report to the production manager on set.
> ➤ Ensure you are pleasant and professional. No one likes a Diva!
> ➤ Do not hold up the production. I advise you to be mindful and considerate. Being helpful will endear you to the people you work with. This aligns with the 7 Spiritual Laws of Success, which will benefit both your career and life.
> ➤ Introduce yourself to the director.
> ➤ Ensure your performance is so well prepared that you do not have to worry about it later. If you are practicing your 4 Agreements you will do your best. You only have one chance before television audiences around the country see you. Remember that what you are doing in that intimate environment will be broadcast by the time you have forgotten it.
> ➤ ALWAYS use your Secret Weapon. You may rest assured that everything is at it should be.
> ➤ Remember to breathe deeply and slowly . . .

Chapter 17

Theatre

Theatre is a true creative and collaborative process. When we enter the story of a play, there is a real sense of Actors merging as an ensemble, to bring truth to this story. My experience of Theatre has varied from working for big mainstream productions and fringe Theatre working in what we call Co-Ops, where Actors work for a percentage of the profits. The difference between film, television and theatre is that with theatre, there is an instant response and connection with the audience. Film and TV are a lot more intimate. In theatre, we achieve intimacy whilst projecting our voices so that our audience can hear us.

Theatre-sports are not only absolutely hilarious and entertaining they are fantastic training for improvisation and placing you out of your comfort zone, in the moment, with incredible results. It is being completely present and open to the realm of all possibility, thinking on your feet. Fringe Theatre is very popular and has developed a very strong reputation in the industry and amongst audiences. The instant reward you receive from an audience is absolutely enthralling. There is nothing quite like "nailing" a scene and moving an audience. There is also a real humility and respect for our craft, in my opinion, because most people working in fringe theatre are doing it for the love of their craft, not the monetary reward. In co-op theatre the profits vary.

When I heard I had an audition for TONY & TINA'S WEDDING I was thrilled. It was a hit off Broadway show. The American Directors were here to work on the Australian Production. The show was unique, in that although it had a structure, most of it was improvised. Not only that, it was set at a church, the audience was escorted back to the Reception Hall on foot and there was a lot of audience participation. When I went for that casting, the first thing I did was hire a wedding dress! After all I wanted to be cast as the bride. At that point I didn't have a car, so on the day of the audition, I was seen running down the street in my sunnies and a wedding dress, being honked by every passing car. When I walked into the audition, I could hardly see a thing. The directors laughed and suggested I take my sunnies off. They were very impressed with my initiative and soon I won the role of Marina, one of the three bridesmaids.

It was a great experience. Each performance went for around three hours; it was quite exhausting. The show was a hit we were filled to capacity every evening. The season ran for a few months, until the company went broke, owing us wages. The case went to Actor's Equity, but our money was never recovered. These things can happen.

Sometimes disasters happen! In FIVE TIMES DIZZY, my agent called and told me the lead actress had dropped out two weeks prior to going on National Tour. I was sent to audition for the lead role and won the role within a day or so. I was offered a contract which would last for five months and take me all around Australia with a great cast of Actors, doing a show for high school students in major Theatres. Theatre South produced this show.

Rehearsals were a whirlwind. I had one week of rehearsals without a set. In Actor's terms, that is jumping into the deep end. Rehearsals usually go for a few weeks and Actors go through 'blocking' scenes on stage and rehearse so much that the play becomes second nature. Then there are dress rehearsals and previews where the director gives Actors final notes, before the show opens to the public and the media. The Media are generally invited to review theatre.

That is not to excuse what I am about to tell you, which happens to be every Actor's nightmare and happened to me. Here goes! This particular play was quite repetitive in language between scenes. Quite often the language of each scene began in a similar fashion. As the lead Actor, I was on stage for every scene except for one or two I recall.

Forgoing previews and the like, it was time to tour to our first destination, which was in Western Australia. Within two weeks I had packed up my life to go on the road and rehearsed the leading role in a play. The curtains opened and the play started. It was all going swimmingly until I cut from the middle of the play, right to the last scene. Within a split second I saw the actors standing in costume stage right and left, suddenly go into panic and start disrobing into different costumes to match the scene I had started. At the end of the auditorium I saw the Director plunge his head into his hands in despair. I quickly realised my mistake but it was too late to go back. The play finished in record time.

That is an experience I beat myself up about for years to come. I had recurring nightmares about it. The rest of the tour was a success and we performed in front of audiences of up to one thousand people around Australia, but that was the one nightmare moment of my Acting Career. I have never felt so much shame and disbelief. I was devastated, but I had to recover quickly as the show had to continue touring. When you are cast in a theatre production, the cliché expression "The Show Must Go On" is true.

Each Theatre Production I participated in had its own story. My first One Woman Show was called A RICH WOMAN'S LAMENT. That was a huge learning curve for me, as I discovered I was the sole Actor responsible for holding the audience's attention. Very quickly I felt the energy of the audience as it stayed with me on my journey as this character, as opposed to dropping the energy on stage and losing the audience in the process. Once the Audience is lost it is very difficult to regain them. Being prone to anxiety, it was a very stressful undertaking and it had its physical toll. Having said that however, it was also the most empowering experience I have ever had as an actor.

At times we are asked to prepare in no time at all. In THE VAGINA MONOLOGUES, again I was cast very quickly and because the cast was so big, we literally only had one day of rehearsal on set at NIDA. That was a cast of thousands; approximately forty Actors participated. It was a very long and very memorable day. Friendships were made and great women worked for a great cause. There are so many stories to tell, but I wanted to cover key aspects, so that you have specific industry examples to draw from. One thing I will say is that art really did imitate life for me in some of the roles I was cast in.

Suggested Choices

➤ When you are requested to prepare an audition piece for a show, ensure you prepare a piece appropriate for the play you are going for. For instance if you were casting for a Shakespeare, you would prepare a classical piece preferably Shakespeare.

➤ Read and know the play you are casting for well, so that you have context and a better idea of the character you are testing for.

➤ Arrive as the character you are casting for in the play.

➤ Connecting with the director is a great advantage, as long as it is an authentic relationship. It is important you trust his/her direction during the rehearsal process. It is strongly advised you do not argue with your director.

➤ In theatre, an ensemble of actors may work together for extended periods. It may become a very close group. Actors are often sad after closing night, as they miss the ensemble.

➤ Refrain from directing fellow Actors. Leave that to the Director, no matter how clearly you see something. If in turn an Actor chooses to direct you, by practicing self-referral you will be able to handle the situation without taking it on board.

➤ If you are under rehearsed, collaborate with your director, rather than let yourself down. Perhaps the Director can schedule some additional rehearsal time for you.

➤ If you throw yourself in the deep end, expect some fall out, but if you do falter, you can pick yourself right up again and go on with the show, doing your best.

➤ "Dropping the Ball" as some of us call it, or dropping the energy in a show can be quite detrimental to a performance. It is a well-known phenomenon on the second night of a show, following Opening Night, when everyone is on such a high.

➤ Ensure you do all you can to maintain your performance at optimum level for every show. Remember you will have a different audience each time and they deserve to see a great show.

➤ If you do happen to experience an Actor's worst nightmare as I did, beating yourself up will not help you as much as forgiving yourself for being human and making a mistake. You will then be best able to detach from the past and perform brilliantly in the future.

➤ Use your Secret Weapon! It is important that you maintain your holistic lifestyle, especially with long-term productions. They can be exhausting.

➤ Remember to keep breathing, deeply and slowly . . .

Five Times Dizzy, Theatre South National Tour

Chapter 18

Commercials

Many actors do not consider commercials to be 'acting'. They do not always challenge one artistically. Nevertheless, in this country, they are generally better paid than Theatre, Television and sometimes Film, if one is a working actor as opposed to a celebrity. Therefore, it makes sense to do them. They are also fun to do. Some Commercial shoots can take hours upon hours and some are very quick and easy. The budgets for Commercials are usually substantial, so the best of everything is provided in terms of catering, locations, wardrobe, make up and the treatment one receives as an Actor, or Talent, a common term used for us, by Advertising. There is also the possibility of working with some very well known directors. I recall working on a Telstra commercial with UK Director Joe Wright, famous for period block-busters.

Over the years I have participated in more commercials than I remember to name for products like paint, banks, taxes, mattresses, telecommunications and the list goes on. The most recent commercial I did was a scene between four women. On the day of the shoot, the parts were yet to be decided. Having learnt all the parts, I knew which one I wanted and which of the parts I could really do justice to. Practicing what I preach, I trusted it would be offered to me and it was. I had a brilliant day, was happy with my work and received great accolades from the client, producer and director. It also turned out to be the starring role in the commercial! I was so grateful to have such a great experience I asked to perform to the best of my ability.

I have had some great experiences, like learning to drive a forklift for a commercial and sitting in a waiting room full of moths in moth season in absolute panic as I have a phobia of them, determined not to let them beat me. That was a wise choice, because I won that commercial. Commercials can also take you away to great places and you can experience all sorts of adventures.

Going for Commercials is different from casting for Television, Film or Theatre. Casting Directors for Commercials usually have many people to see in one day, one after the other in fifteen-minute intervals. Actors are usually given three takes to get the scene right, in front of the camera. Then the tapes are sent to the Director and the short list is chosen for a call-back. Call-backs can be great, for instance on a Dulux commercial, they only wanted to call me back to help them choose a partner for me, so there was no competition! Sometimes however, the stakes can be very high, especially if the commercial is worth a lot of money.

Commercials have given me opportunities to do a lot. In the year 2000 I was very fortunate to have four commercials on air at once. That bestowed me the budget to take a European Vacation. Within two weeks I arranged to travel for six months. That was an amazing experience.

Travelling was the most amazing gift I had ever given myself. I relished every moment. The most significant outcome of my overseas trip was the realisation there was a whole world out there. It was the first time I truly experienced what was a very significant lesson. I realised I was so obsessed with Acting I had tunnel vision. Arriving back in Australia, I decided to re-evaluate my life and create more balance.

I do hope you can see the value of leading a well-balanced, holistic life as an artist. Artists are known to disappear for weeks at a time when they are in the process of creation. In my case, the realisation didn't hit until my mid 30s! The reason I have been repetitive in making suggestions to you about your inner life is to emphasise the importance of making inner work as significant as the work you do on your craft. It is after all, directly related to your work.

Chapter 19

Your Secret Weapon!

So far, you have learnt how to enter into and operate in the industry, following a healthy approach. What this chapter will teach you is how to give yourself an edge and empower you as an Actor or Artist in your work and your life. I will introduce you to the idea of being a Deliberate Creator, something that takes discipline, practice and dedication and the Most Important Thing You Will Ever Do! It may sound like work, but wait until you see it working before your very eyes, it is life changing. Once you gain experience of manifesting you will be so excited, I imagine you will manifest more and more.

The trick is consistency, repetition. If you commit to it, you will discover magic.

Over the years, through my journey of personal growth and my fascination with the human condition and study of inspirational material, I have learnt to manifest things quickly. I have had experiences where I have created situations exactly matching my vision. I didn't realise that what I was actually doing was creating.

I was creating unconsciously. In making films, I was fulfilling visions and I started learning how to create things deliberately. Over the years of my wonderful inner discovery, I learnt that we have the power to be the masters of our own Universe and I can personally vouch for it. As I learnt more and more on the subject, I practiced deliberate manifestation, with astounding results. Since then I have manifested things daily. You could say that I am a product of all the work I recommend to you.

There is no doubt that my own journey was one of trial and error and that while most people go through life changes at random, I have experienced big changes on a regular basis! Only three months ago I lost my TV Hosting job, home and car in the space of a couple of weeks, through no fault of my own. This would be an incredibly stressful time for anyone who is not yet awake. In my mind, the Universe decided to clear my slate of everything that didn't work for me! After the initial shock, I started thinking about what I would love! One of the thoughts I had was, I would love to live in a beautiful big house with friends and guess what happened? Just that! I now live in a rock star house/mansion. Further, I have had use of my friend's car, which is eco friendly and I am currently snowed under with all the work I love.

I was once told it was like I was dropped onto this earth and thrown into the deep end! What an amazing gift! Many of you may be horrified and I ask you to consider this: every perceived obstacle or mishap is an opportunity to grow and expand. Hence, I am the recipient of a wealth of experience and expansion. There is never a day I forget to be grateful.

I am living PROOF that this practice works!

THE POWER OF DELIBERATE CREATION!

This practice will not only allow you to experience only that which you want to experience and appreciate that which you don't. It will empower you as a person in your acting or creative career, for it gives you a certainty and security that cannot be shaken in any situation. Your Secret Weapon will give you Certainty over Uncertainty.

If you follow the recommendations I have made for you in this book, there is no doubt you will master Self Referral and Authenticity. You will also absorb great values. Your imagination is the only limit to your success.

Authors like Eckhart Tolle, Wallace D. Wattles, Napoleon Hill, Esther and Jerry Hicks, William Fezller Ph.D, Barry Gross, Dr Wayne Dyer are but a few of the teachers of Your Secret Weapon.

Dr Wayne Dyer's AH meditations are an excellent way of starting your day, creating that which you focus on. Is there anything more powerful than our Imagination? Guided meditation will make your process of creation easier. You will be asked to visualise and feel that which you would like to manifest and guided all the way to the completion of your dream, with the knowledge that it is in the process of realisation and your work is done! The more you trust the process as you go along, the more creative you can become with your visualisations and the more you realise that the sky is the limit! Dr Wayne Dyer's AH meditations are great if you like to be guided along. Another meditation I can recommend which takes you years into the future is Kelly Howell's guided healing meditation. It works on the left and right brain coupled with circular breathing, it is amazing. I tend to travel in a constant space of creative visualisation.

So here is the Practice! It entails going into a meditative state and letting your imagination run wild as you visualise yourself in any desired situation. You can visualise absolutely anything. I advise you to focus on one thing at a time. You then feel the amazing joy and gratitude as you experience your dreams in the meditation. When you come back to the room, you can feel assured that it has gone out to the Universe and it is on its way to you. As you learn to trust that, you are better able to detach and get out of your own way. Repetition works well, if there is something specific you would love. An Oscar for instance, may take a little longer than a new abode. This is how we, as creative souls, move from uncertainty into certainty. Along with Self Referral it is the difference between heaven and hell in my experience.

All your Dreams will unfold easily and effortlessly. Can you imagine that? Breathing deeply, slowly, all the time, connects you to your Source and releases any resistance to your dreams. The more you connect to your Source, the more creative you become, the more authentic you become and the more connected you become. We are all connected! Feeling that eliminates any feeling of separation and you are able to extend the same love you have for yourself to others. You deserve to be all of who you are there is absolutely no reason to play small! As you connect to your source through meditation, you will experience the magnitude of your power. Louise Hay equates breathing with taking life in. Is there any reason you would deny breathing life in fully?

No matter how dark you perceive a situation to be, know that you have a choice to turn things around at any moment and an easy way to do that is to be thankful. If you find it hard to give thanks because "there is nothing to be grateful for", how about the air you breathe or the food you have to eat today? Dr Dyer's OM meditations are perfect for giving thanks. It is a great way to relax at the end of the day before you go to sleep. Dr Deepak Chopra's 7 Spiritual Laws of Success are something I will never tire of listening to. What a relief to quiet the mind of judgement for instance. You are your attention; why not turn your attention to that which gives you joy!

Know that your thoughts create your reality and your words are very powerful. It would follow that you may like to be aware of what you are thinking and what you are saying. Let me give you an example: If you have a habit of complaining in your conversations, what message is that sending out? On the other hand, what if you just focussed on what you love and what makes you happy? Food for thought. It is the combination of what I have suggested to you that will create Magic in your life as an Artist. Make this a daily practice. The trick is consistency. Start small and as you gain confidence you can Create Anything!

Now I will tell you about the power of stating intentions. The power of stating intentions along with creative visualisation is dynamite!

What is Intention?

The power of the word is magic. When you make a statement, the Universe goes to work to realise it. If you trust this, you have the power to create every situation, as you would like it. An intention may be as simple as "I intend to be fully focussed today", "I intend to travel to my destination in Perfect time" or "I intend to perform brilliantly today and win my audition". You can break down your entire day and state your intentions for each action every morning. Then you can relax and let it all unfold, knowing you have put the preparation in.

I recommend you begin each day with what I call a ritual, where you manifest your day. Do the meditations daily and then state your intentions.

Your vision as an artist is your key to fulfilling your soul purpose. If you follow my suggestions, keep the vision strong and chip away at it every day, it will unfold for you at the perfect time. Know that you are at the perfect place in your life at every moment. The trick is consistency. Consider the inner work you do as part of the work you do for your brand daily. Couple that with a healthy diet and exercise invest in your relationships and your loved ones and you achieve balance and magic!

Hosting Psychic TV

Chapter 20

How To LOVE not DREAD Auditions

I would now like to gift you with The Number 1 VITAL Audition Tip, The most important of all Audition Tips you will ever need to know.

Why? Because it will alter your perception of the entire Audition experience and make your Dreams Come True!

Ok, so you've got an Audition, the Stakes are high, you really want it, and it's your Dream come true, the Competition is fierce; if you don't get this you will just die! Sound familiar?

The one thing I keep hearing from Actors and Professionals alike is that they "Dread" Auditions. The word out there is that Auditions are something to be feared and let's face it, when you really want something, when it means everything to you, of course it will make you a little anxious to say the least! That is the time we really put ourselves out there to be judged on our merit, it is extremely important to us. I have gone to Networking Sessions and heard Professionals speak to budding young Actors, telling them that Auditions are scary! That's a nice way to mould Creative Souls isn't it?

So what do we do?

Well, generally and unfortunately we tend to go into all our limiting beliefs and fears. Are we prepared enough, who else is going for it, the classic "I never get ads, or films or TV shows", they are better than me, the casting director didn't like me, I never get my dream jobs, I am not attractive or thin enough and the list goes on and on.

Anyone ever notice how we attract our fears? We say or think negative things and then congratulate ourselves for being 'right' when they happen, painful as that may be, all the while not realizing that we are making choices every second and that we fulfil our own prophecies! That is why it is absolutely imperative that we are practicing our Secret Weapon!

So how can we go from Dreading Auditions to Loving Them?

As Actors or Entertainers we LOVE our Work, our creativity feeds our soul, otherwise why would we do it right?

So here it is are you READY?

What if you had an audition for something you would die and go to heaven for and instead of going into panic and dread you changed your mindset?

How, you may ask? Apart from using Your Secret Weapon, As Actors, we use our imagination don't we? The trick to LOVING Auditions is simple: Go to your Audition with the real Belief that You are actually on set, on stage, on location, playing the role your are auditioning for!

So if it's Theatre, picture yourself in front of the Audience, if its Stage, likewise, if its TV or Film, in front of the Camera knowing there are millions of viewers watching you and loving your Performance.

You LOVE Performing! Can you imagine a better experience?

So that's it, simple isn't it? Imagine your Audition to be Your Awarding Winning Performance in the actual Role.

Guess what? That also sends a message to the Universe to make it happen for you, so it's a double whammy! So what are you waiting for? Start LOVING AUDITIONS!

Chapter 21

Your Brand

Welcome to your Brand! By now you have some idea of what being a brand entails. I would now like to provide you with more detail. If we are selling a product, it follows we like it to be immaculate. Further we would like to give it its true value. We would also benefit from marketing it; hence our Brand must be marketable. After all, when we shop would we buy a less than perfect product?

Here is a prime example of the creation of a Brand: Dita Von Teese has made Burlesque and herself famous worldwide. Burlesque is now very popular, largely due to her work. When Dita was young, she entered into a rather trashy strip joint in the States, searching for work. As she entered the club, she noticed it was filled with blond, busty, tanned exotic dancers. Many people would think, "I don't fit in here". Dita was petite, brunette with alabaster skin. What is inspiring about Dita is that instead of thinking she didn't belong, she saw an opportunity to bring something different. She knew her unique talent and she saw a market for it. That is the definition of what a Brand is. It is bringing your unique talent to life.

Before the birth of the Internet and worldwide exposure, actors and artists generally adhered to the status quo. They were relatively powerless to the Industry as it operated. Allow me to explain. Regardless of which countries we are in, we were historically subject to competition, rejection, typecasting, trends and of course agents, casting directors, directors and producers. The Industry still exists and operates in such a manner today. Hence as you enter the Industry you will be expected to play 'by the rules'.

Wherever you are in your career as an artist, the technology available to us today will allow you to promote your Brand. It means you can operate inside and outside the square. It is outside the square you can create a real brand, because you have absolute creative control over it. It is Your Choice! Your Brand is the way you would like the world to perceive you. I found I was typecast for years in the Industry, where making my own films and working in independent film allowed me to be creatively fulfilled. Since filming Touch ups with Tula and presenting on Television, I have truly begun to promote my own unique talent and Brand, as I would like it.

By practicing the inner work I suggest for you, you will become aware of your own unique talent. There is something very special about every single one of us, something we can offer as a service to the world. As you tap in to your true nature and expression and ask what service you are here to provide, your unique talent will be obvious to you. The inspiration you gain through mediation and visualisation will put you on the right path to fulfil your purpose.

Your Brand includes how you look! You may choose a look that best expresses your Brand and stay with that. Musicians for example are known to exhibit distinct costumes, hairstyles and make up. If you are an Actor, you may choose a character you love and promote that as your Brand. This is not to say that you will have to stick to one character. You may decide to promote different characters as part of your Brand. If you are a comic you will have a specific style as a Brand. If you are an artist, your paintings will generally be of a particular genre.

In my journey as an Actor, I have worked in theatre, film, television and commercials. I have however met prominent actors who choose to focus only on film, or television and do not accept work in theatre for example. If you love theatre, there is no harm in placing all your attention on that. My focus is now on television for example.

Marketing your Brand includes uploading videos on the internet, using social media, blogging, sending links to casting directors by email and having your own website. The more you blog, using key words Google will pick up, the higher you will rank on Google. When you do build a following on your blog, generally advertisers become interested and you can create a passive income for yourself. Further, your Brand extends to every contact you have with the public. If you go out in your unique style, people become interested and you are able to let them know what you do, which will create more followers for you. That is why your product must be immaculate.

As you build your profile independently the Industry begins to take notice and you are then offered work that suits you specifically. It gives you credibility. So if you love singing, sing! If you love acting, act! If you love dancing, dance! You are constantly stating your intention to the Universe.

Daily Diary:

> - Begin your day with your Secret Weapon, in meditation.
> - State your intentions for the day
> - Exercise
> - Ensure you eat well. Eating non-processed food, staying away from fried food, wheat, sugar, fatty cheeses etc. will benefit you with a light feeling and make you happier.
> - Work on your craft. If you are working on several projects at once, it is wise to manage your time well.
> - Always give yourself leisure time to enjoy your loved ones.
> - End the day in Gratitude for all that you are and all that you have.

If you do keep a diary, you will better be able to have a healthy balance so that your body, mind and spirit are fulfilled.

We live in a very exciting age of growing awareness and excellence in technology and science. We are becoming more and more powerful as we realise the God in all of us. I hope that you now have a better idea about how you can create your Brand.

Chapter 22

Your Website

Your website should reflect your Brand and be a great representation for you. Portfolios previously consisted of hardcopy black and white headshots, a hardcopy biography and show reels sent by post. Today your Portfolio is your Website, as everything operates electronically. So here's how you can create your website in the most cost efficient and fun way!

> ➢ Step 1: Compile elements for your website. You will need a Biography with your credits listed including date, role, production, director and producer. If you are still studying, you may list productions you have participated in at your drama institution. Next, you will need a headshot. This should look like you, so that casting directors can refer to your photo and expect to see you looking that way. Actors generally update their headshots every one or two years. You will then need to collect any footage you have for your website, including your show reel. Show reels should be 2-3 minutes in length, without intros or montage sequences, scenes are preferable and boys screaming and girls crying in scenes are taboo. Then you will film a welcome video for your home page. This can be a little 30-60 second "Thank you for visiting my website", just showing a little of your

personality and putting you in front of the camera, which is after all what you do! These days you can use a smart phone to video anything and the quality is great. If you also do voice over work and have a reel you should include that.

➤ Your Website Pages should include a Home Page, About, Blog, Footage/reel, Stills, Media, Contact. On your Home page you will have your welcome video as well as a little paragraph about yourself and what you love written in third person. Every actor should blog or vlog. Write about what you are doing and post videos on your blog regularly. You will be surprised how many people will be interested and attracted to your website. If you don't yet have any media for that page, you can always say "Stay Tuned". Your Contact Page should consist of a form visitors to your site fill in, not your personal details! If an Agent represents you, you may also list the agency as a contact.

➤ The Website: There are free websites with some great templates you can just fill in, like Wordpress or Wix for example. So unless you are unable to fill in the templates and design it yourself, it shouldn't cost you anything. If you have a budget, its great if you can employ a web designer to do a professional site for you. Next you will need a domain name and you can Google domain hosts. Your domain name should be www.yourname.com. Always choose .com if you can. Once you are happy with the design of your site and you have bought your domain name, which is a nominal fee for a few years, you are ready to Publish your site to the world! To do that you need a domain host, like Hostgator for instance and it costs under $10 a month. If you visit my site there is a Hostgator icon on the right and apparently you will receive a discount if you click on that. I am not advertising Hostgator by the way, its just one I know.

So there you have it, your Brand is out on your very own Website and it doesn't cost much at all. Its actually fun designing your site! There are many Industry Networks on the net. Once you are up and running, you can connect with them and promote your brand. This includes social marketing. You can create many employment opportunities on the Internet. I suggest you spend some time researching and connecting with those networks; it will be of huge benefit to you. You can also write or comment on other people's blogs, which will bring attention to your brand. The possibilities are endless.

Chapter 23

Agents, Contracts
and Industrial Affairs

Your Agent will handle the business of acting, such as contracts, negotiations, deal memos, call sheets, wardrobe calls etc. There are times however when you may find yourself going freelance. In Australia we have the MEAA, or Media, Entertainment, Arts Alliance. They constitute our Union.

If you are not represented for a time, these organisations will have standard industry contracts and provide helpful resources to you. It is advisable to join your Union, as they are there to regulate, improve and protect wages, working conditions and the rights of their members. They provide legal representation, strive to attain sexual and racial equality, regulate questions of professional ethics, training and education, financial assistance in hardship, alert members of misbehaving stakeholders and the list goes on.

Not that long ago I entered into a verbal agreement through a friend to present advertorials on television. When their end of the agreement wasn't honoured, had a contract been in place, I would have been in a much better position. It is my experience that when producers do not wish to go through agents or our union it is because they do not wish to honour what we do.

There is much legality in our Industry and it can be quite complicated, hence it is advisable to have good representation. I am happy to leave all that to my agent to deal with!

On another occasion, when the off Broadway Show "Tony and Tina's Wedding" went bust, we were not paid our wages. The matter went to the Alliance and they were involved in recovering the monies owed to the cast and crew.

I do suggest that if you go freelance, you carefully research the companies you become involved with. If you do enter into agreements, please ensure you have signed contracts and negotiations and there is nothing left to question. If you are using your Secret Weapon and all the tools I have bestowed you with, you will always be in a great place to deal with things as they come up.

Epilogue

In this book I have continued to repeat certain themes, such as self-referral and authenticity, good values, focussing on your quality of life and balance, getting to know and love yourself, your craft and your industry. I have also stressed stating your Intentions and learning the Art of Creation. It is Crucial you use Your Secret Weapon Daily if you would like magic to be a part of your life. Aligning with Your Spirit will not only give you an edge in your Career, it will give you an extraordinary life. Your Creative Self is equally important as your Brand as an Actor.

The life of an Actor is a magical gift of discovery and experience. I can honestly say I have had an extraordinary life and I am very fortunate, as are all those who follow their soul purpose. We are all wealthy in our own way and that is determined by the values we hold dearest and closest to our hearts.

Sharing details about my illness has been a difficult feat, as it is my spirit that I identify with. I did it with the motivation to illuminate you as you begin your journey as an actor, to nurture your craft and nurture yourself at the same time. I am now successfully changing my body blueprint and have already eliminated certain health issues. As it happens, my illness has been a great gift, because it has given me the time to develop my creative projects and pursue my creative dreams. It has also taught me to nurture myself. I know that for you, there is a simpler way to do that, by practicing deliberate Creation and living a Spiritual and Creative life. I am by no means a Master, only a student. The great news is, in this book you can reap the rewards of a journey of many years.

As Actors we are faced with different situations all the time. I have learned that Change is the only certainty in life. In this knowledge we are open to all magical possibility.

Acting is a vocation for those who wish to grow and explore and discover. It is a lifestyle and a life pursuit. That is what it means to me. As a Deliberate Creator, please remember to express your gratitude and show humility. It is something you will find most successful people do! I imagine you will find it easy to be grateful as you experience more and more magic in your career and life. If you are fulfilling your life purpose you will naturally dwell in spirit, rather than the ego.

As Dr Deepak Chopra would say, "If you are living in Uncertainty, you are on the right track"

I hope "The Truth About Acting" has been helpful to you and I wish you amazing success. There is nothing I would love more than to see you Thrive! May you live in a state of Inspiration!

Love and Light,
Tula Tzoras